EXTREME

ugs

Trevor Day

Produced for A & C Black by

MONKEY PUZZLE MEDIA LTD

Monkey Puzzle Media Ltd
48 York Avenue
Hove BN3 1PJ, UK

Published by A & C Black Publishers Limited
36 Soho Square, London W1D 3QY

Paperback published 2009
First published 2008
Copyright © 2008 A & C Black Publishers Limited

ISBN 978-1-4081-0016-5 (hardback)
ISBN 978-1-4081-0093-6 (paperback)

The right of Trevor Day to be identified as the
author of this Work has been asserted by him in
accordance with the Copyright, Designs and Patents
Act 1988.

A CIP catalogue record for this book is available
from the British Library.

Editor: Steve Parker
Design: Mayer Media Ltd
Picture research: Laura Barwick
Series consultant: Jane Turner

This book is produced using paper that is made
from wood grown in managed, sustainable forests.
It is natural, renewable and recyclable. The logging
and manufacturing processes conform to the
environmental regulations of the country of origin.

Printed in China by C & C Offset Printing Co., Ltd

Picture acknowledgements
Alamy p. 6 (Phototake Inc); Bridgeman Art Library
p. 26 (Archives Charmet); Corbis pp. 4 bottom
(MedicalRF.com), 14 top (Visuals Unlimited), 14
bottom (image100), 17 (Mediscan), 19 (Visuals
Unlimited), 20 (CDC/PHIL); Getty Images pp. 5
(Mark Scott), 8 (David Scharf), 12 (Hepp), 13 (Wolf
Fahrenbach), 15 (Dr David M Phillips), 18 (Nicole
Duplaix/National Geographic), 29 (Jan Greune);
Science Photo Library pp. 1 (National Cancer
Institute), 4 top (Andrew Syred), 7 (Steve
Gschmeissner), 9, 10 (Dr Steve Patterson), 11
(Dr John Brackenbury), 16 (Scott Camazine), 21
(Eye of Science), 23 (National Cancer Institute),
24 top (Eye of Science), 24 bottom (Eric Grave),
25 (CNRI), 28; Still Pictures pp. 22 (Darlyne A
Murawski), 27 (Mark Edwards).

The front cover shows a picture of a human head
louse taken through a powerful microscope (Science
Photo Library/Photo Insolité Realité).

Every effort has been made to contact copyright
holders of material reproduced in this book. Any
omissions will be rectified in subsequent printings if
notice is given to the publishers.

CONTENTS

Abbreviations **m** stands for metres • **ft** stands for feet • **in** stands for inches •
cm stands for centimetres • **km/h** stands for kilometres per hour • **mph** stands for miles per hour

Nice home!

Your body is like a snack bar on legs for all kinds of creatures, from tiny microbes to tapeworms many metres long!

Your body is a great place to live. It has hideaways that are warm and moist, and contain food for body **bugs** of all shapes and sizes. You carry around some of these bugs all the time. Others are only occasional visitors — but the worst could kill you.

At 1,000 times real size, a pin's sharp point looks blunt — and it's covered with the kinds of microbes that get on and in the body.

Tiny critters

Your body is made up of 100 billion **cells** – plus 20 microscopic bugs for each cell!

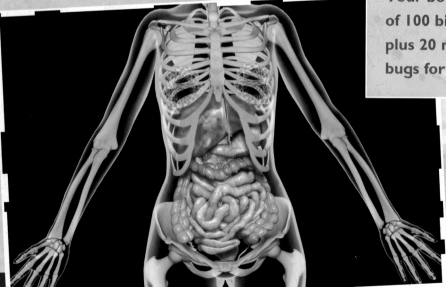

This is what your guts look like! Worms inside a person's guts can grow longer than a bus!

bug general name for any microscopic or small animal

The mouth is one of the body's dirtiest places.

Head lice roam through the forest of hair, sucking blood as they go.

Even happy, healthy people are home to body bugs!

The nose breathes in tiny floating bugs.

Armpits are a great place for smelly microbes to live.

Miniature fungi (related to mushrooms) can grow between toes.

cells microscopic structures that make up living things

5

Feeling lousy?

**Head itching? Needs a scratch?
You could be feeling the effects of
hundreds of lousy suckers.**

Head lice are tiny **insect parasites** that live on
people's scalps. These miniature vampires suck your
blood. They are half the size of this "o" and hard to
spot. They can even change colour to match your
hair. Sharing hats, combs or hair brushes, or just
touching heads, can help lice move from one
person to another.

The louse leaves
droppings all over
the skin and hairs.

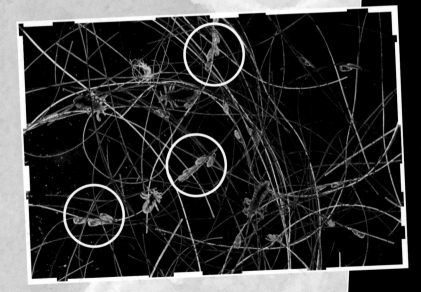

Louse eggs (nits) stick tightly to hairs.

insect small, six-legged animal with a hard outer casing

Lousy

Today the word lousy means "not well", but it originally meant louse-filled!

The louse's mouth is designed to pierce through skin into the scalp and inject saliva.

The saliva stops blood clotting, so the louse can suck it up easily.

Sharp claws dig into skin.

A louse grabs a hair with its six legs. It can crawl but not jump or fly.

parasite creature that lives in or on another creature and does it harm

Open wide

Next time you're tempted to skip brushing your teeth, remember that you're encouraging the bugs that cause stinky breath and rotting teeth!

Plaque is a gunky mixture of *bacteria* and rotting food on teeth, that looks messy under the microscope.

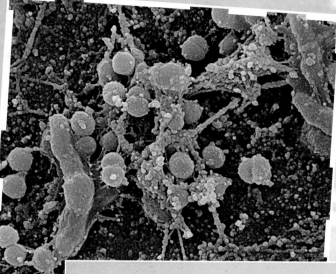

Gums become swollen and tender from acids and other bacterial chemicals.

Long in the tooth

This phrase means "getting old". It describes how the gums shrink back and expose more of the teeth in older people. It is caused by bacterial gum disease.

plaque mixture of bacteria, saliva and rotting food that coats teeth and gums

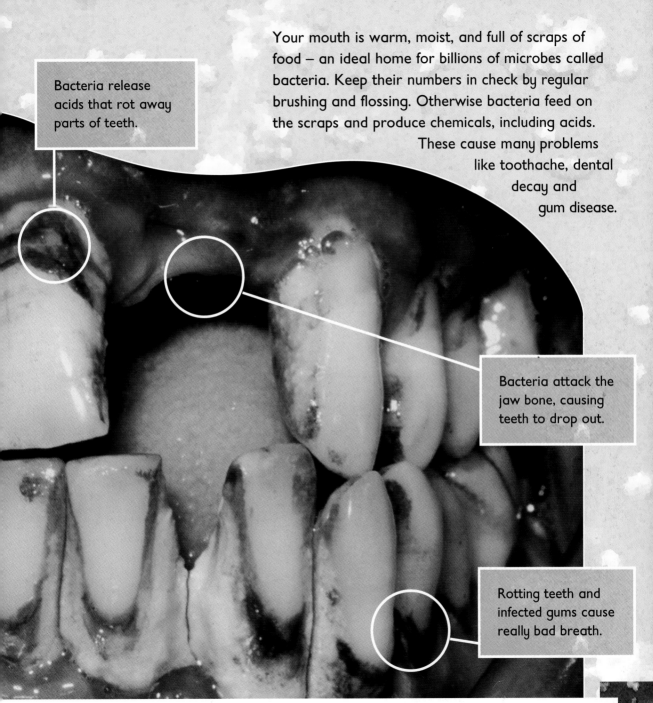

Bacteria release acids that rot away parts of teeth.

Your mouth is warm, moist, and full of scraps of food — an ideal home for billions of microbes called bacteria. Keep their numbers in check by regular brushing and flossing. Otherwise bacteria feed on the scraps and produce chemicals, including acids. These cause many problems like toothache, dental decay and gum disease.

Bacteria attack the jaw bone, causing teeth to drop out.

Rotting teeth and infected gums cause really bad breath.

bacteria common small- to medium-sized microbes

9

Mucus anyone?

Lots of microscopic bugs float in air. Until, that is, you breathe them into their new home – your nose!

Breathed-in microbes first have to get through your tangle of nose hairs. Then they hit sticky slime, called **mucus**, which traps them. Microscopic hairs sweep the mucus to the back of your nose, where you swallow it into your stomach. Here the natural stomach acid kills most of the microbes. Unless, that is, you pick your nose, or blow your mucus – snot – into a handkerchief.

Spray!

Mucus droplets are laden with microbes.

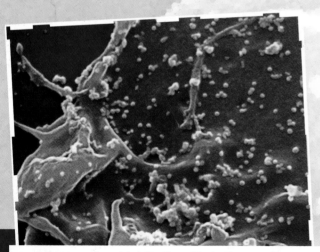

*Common colds are caused by microbes called **viruses** (yellow dots), which are even tinier than bacteria. Viruses and bacteria that make us ill are often called germs.*

mucus natural body slime that gives a slippery, protective coating

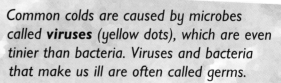

Atchoo! A sneeze propels thousands of mucus droplets from the nose.

Snotty!

In someone with a bad cold, microbes turn the mucus green.

Drip, drip

A nose drips more on a cold day because moisture in the air inside the nose turns from gas to liquid, making the mucus runnier than normal.

Speedy!

Sneezes have been clocked at more than 160 km/h (100 mph)!

virus tiny bug that causes diseases by invading and killing body cells

Sniffing you out!

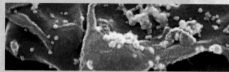

Each person has their own special smell. It's created by the blend of chemicals in their sweat plus a personal mix of microscopic body bugs growing in it!

Bacteria on skin feed on skin flakes and oils. As they grow in stale sweat, they create a stinky smell. We all leave an unseen trail of this odour wherever we go. Even if it is not obvious to us, dogs and some other animals can smell it. Of course, some people are much smellier than others.

*In adults, fresh sweat contains body chemicals called **pheromones**, that may attract people of the opposite sex.*

pheromone chemical that has a smell that affects other people, without them being aware

When sweat evaporates (changes to gas) it cools the skin.

A microscopic view of skin shows its tiny ridges.

Tiny sweat drops ooze from ducts (tubes) onto the skin.

Sweat is mostly water, plus salt, a dash of oil, and urea (a waste substance also found in **urine**).

Beat the whiff

The best ways to get rid of body smells are to wash yourself and your clothes regularly, and use a deodorant.

urine person's liquid waste, also called pee

Fighting invasion!

Your body is always being bombarded by armies of microscopic bugs that try to sneak inside. But you have amazing defences on the outside and inside to keep them at bay.

Your skin is your first line of defence. If a wound or cut lets bugs break through, you could be in trouble. Bacteria called *Staphylococcus* can cause blisters, blood poisoning, or even kill you.

BACTERIA BOUNCE OFF

Dead skin cells form a protective barrier that keeps out bacteria (shown here as pink dots). As old cells rub off, more cells from living layers below rise to take their place.

***Pus** is a pale ooze that forms at a wound and mixes with blood. It shows that white blood cells have been in action, killing bacteria.*

pus pale liquid containing dead blood cells and bacteria

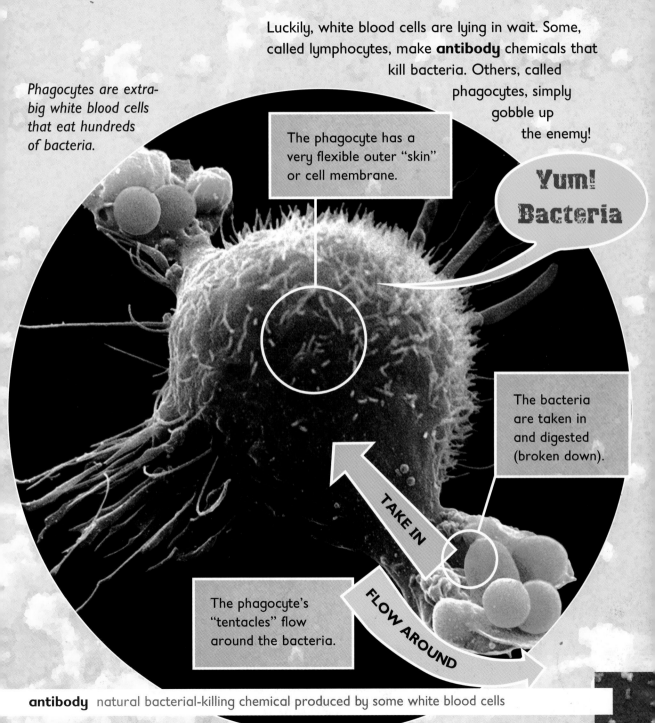

Luckily, white blood cells are lying in wait. Some, called lymphocytes, make **antibody** chemicals that kill bacteria. Others, called phagocytes, simply gobble up the enemy!

Phagocytes are extra-big white blood cells that eat hundreds of bacteria.

The phagocyte has a very flexible outer "skin" or cell membrane.

Yum! Bacteria

The bacteria are taken in and digested (broken down).

TAKE IN

FLOW AROUND

The phagocyte's "tentacles" flow around the bacteria.

antibody natural bacterial-killing chemical produced by some white blood cells

Ticked off

If you go down to the woods today ... be careful what latches onto you. It could be a blood-sucking tick.

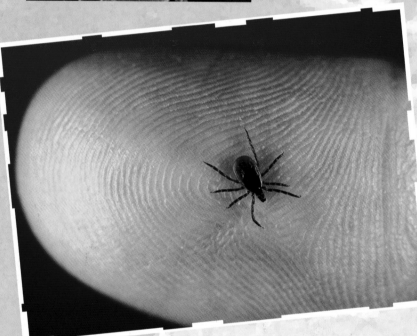

Ticks are not fussy about where they get their blood. A deer tick will just as happily feast on you as on a deer. The trouble is that you could catch a nasty disease in the process. It might be Lyme disease, or maybe Q **fever**, or even Rocky Mountain spotted fever, with **symptoms** like a red skin rash.

Ticks are eight-legged relatives of spiders. A hungry deer tick like this is the size of a match head. Its body swells about ten times larger after a blood meal.

Lyme disease

Effects of Lyme disease include reddening around the tick bite, followed by fever, headache and tiredness, aching muscles and painful joints.

fever high body temperature

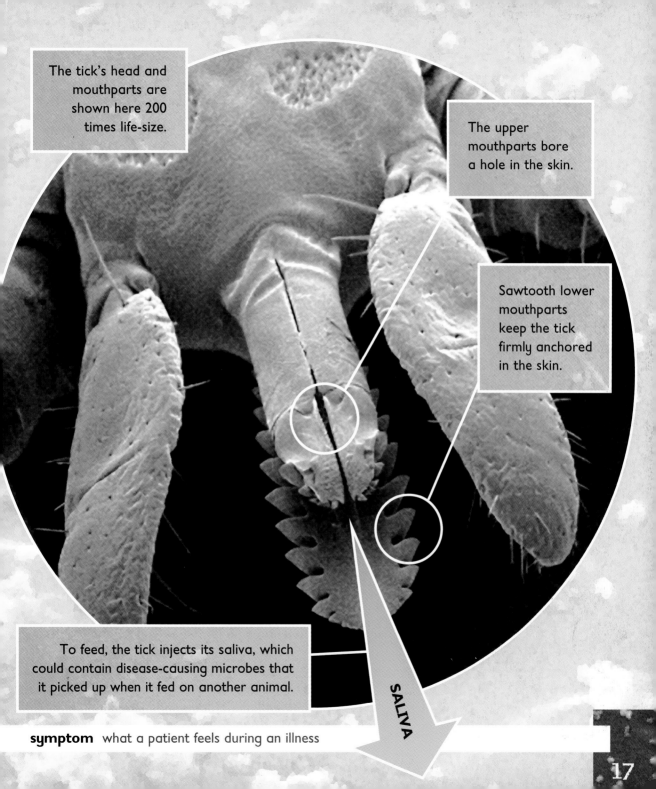

The tick's head and mouthparts are shown here 200 times life-size.

The upper mouthparts bore a hole in the skin.

Sawtooth lower mouthparts keep the tick firmly anchored in the skin.

To feed, the tick injects its saliva, which could contain disease-causing microbes that it picked up when it fed on another animal.

SALIVA

symptom what a patient feels during an illness

A flea in your ear

The Black Death

In Europe and Asia during the 1300s, about 50 million people died from a bacterial disease called bubonic **plague** – the Black Death. It was carried and spread by rat fleas.

What can jump 100 times its own body length, move objects 20,000 times its own weight, and has babies that eat their parents' poo? A flea!

Fleas are blood-sucking insects. Cats and dogs carry fleas, and humans have their own kind too. Fleas have incredibly powerful legs and easily leap from one person to another. By harnessing the natural behaviour of these insects, flea trainers can make them perform tricks in a miniature circus.

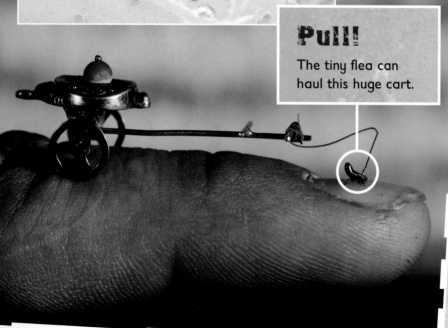

Pull!

The tiny flea can haul this huge cart.

Flea trainers put their performers to sleep briefly and tie them into miniature harnesses.

plague fast-spreading disease that kills people

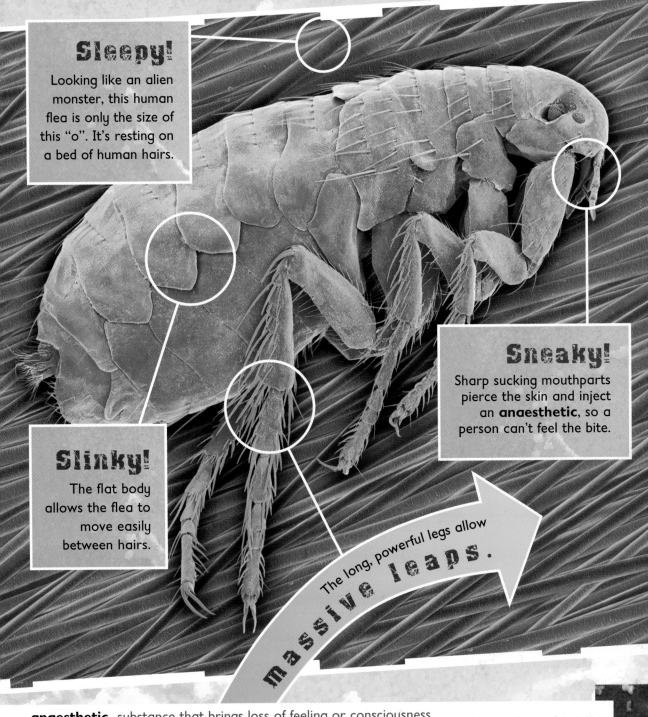

Sleepy!

Looking like an alien monster, this human flea is only the size of this "o". It's resting on a bed of human hairs.

Sneaky!

Sharp sucking mouthparts pierce the skin and inject an **anaesthetic**, so a person can't feel the bite.

Slinky!

The flat body allows the flea to move easily between hairs.

The long, powerful legs allow **massive leaps.**

anaesthetic substance that brings loss of feeling or consciousness

It's in the blood

One small sucker kills more than a million people a year. In some tropical countries the mosquito's bite carries the deadly disease malaria.

Before feeding, the mosquito injects anaesthetic saliva that may contain malaria parasites.

Sharp tube-like mouthparts jab into the skin.

Body **swells** with sucked-up blood.

malaria dangerous disease caused by one-celled parasites transmitted through mosquito bites